THINKING …

Jason Allen-Paisant is from a village called Coffee Grove in Manchester, Jamaica. He is Lecturer in Caribbean Poetry & Decolonial Thought in the School of English at the University of Leeds, where he is also the Director of the Institute for Colonial and Postcolonial Studies. He serves on the editorial board of *Callaloo: Journal of African Diaspora Arts and Letters*. He holds a doctorate in Medieval and Modern Languages from the University of Oxford, and he speaks seven languages. He lives in Leeds.

THINKING WITH TREES

Jason Allen-Paisant

CARCANET POETRY

First published in Great Britain in 2021 by
Carcanet
Alliance House, 30 Cross Street
Manchester, M2 7AQ
www.carcanet.co.uk

Text copyright © Jason Allen-Paisant 2021

The right of Jason Allen-Paisant to be identified as the author
of this work has been asserted in accordance with the
Copyright, Designs and Patents Act of 1988; all rights reserved.

A CIP catalogue record for this book is
available from the British Library.

ISBN 978 1 80017 113 8

Book design by Andrew Latimer
Printed in Great Britain by SRP Ltd, Exeter, Devon

The publisher acknowledges financial
assistance from Arts Council England.

CONTENTS

For Keturah, as ever, my reason for writing

CROSSING THE THRESHOLD

I am walking
I am not going

my body moves along the way
with patience for the breeze

the morning pallor
lies on the green the

ravens stand
on the light and

the expanse opens
to my feet

*

high pitch and stitching
sound of the jackdaws

a bedding of brown leaves
covering the humus

and in the middle
is a stream

that can hardly be heard
I come up from the round

water with shadows
I did not know

*

I can smell spring rising
from the soft hollow

the stream
hides things

under its mirror
whispers

growths
blood

skin coming
to cover the body

It flows more heavily
in a black bed

leaves Banana Ground
the crack

where home runs
where yam vines settle

on a silent river
through a hill

of steep bones
singing

from all sides
through the woodland

I hear Damn Head
cow pastures and tomato beds

more loudly
over brown leaves so alive

so alive
the ground is

a black dress falling on a bed
of pure manure

green shoots are out
the ivy floor gives off

murmured laughs
and a bird shoots

through the tangled
thoroughfare

what does the stream in Coffee Grove
feel as it grows near?

*

going deeper now into the
intimate recesses of the trunk

into the zones hidden
from view

but working
to keep me alive

my eye looking at me
from everywhere

and making noises
the forest refusing to

quiet its walking
eyes of the

hillside
in black soil

sounds
in the redness of barks

the dangling of the branches
in the brain of the stream

*

faceless tree whose eyes dip
into muddy tracks

I have space for you in
my blood

within you
shines a flame

travelling under your dress
the sap flowing

in your inner dark
are the words I want

the words
of a classroom of trees

*

three teenagers are young-
ing their lives

on the crest of the hill
highlights of orange

spill
down on

their laughs
the sunset

with a trail of jet smoke
over the clearing

a Black man comes through
a thicket

with his baby   gives the head tilt
yeah bra

seeing
me see him

here in the woods
the darkness encloses just right

I go towards the tangled arch
not far away

my volumes enter
a cell

In it I hear
the sound of protoplasm

bursting
the green grass

coming back
at my feet

as I walk

*

but what are these woods
anyway?

I do not always understand
what changes inside my head

when the muscle boys with pit bulls
and knives appear

If the city is so hostile then
why would we come here

where nobody would find us
if we were mauled

if we lay bleeding
a densely covered tree would hide us

in here
history keeps following me around

so to be in these woods
is not your idea of being free

but you will keep on
seeing me

*

a sprout of grass
in a root's crevice

blooms into a pack
of dogs

beware of spring
believe you are

a sprout of grass
and love all you see

but come out of the woods
before the white boys

with pitbulls
come

*

the barks
in winter

solid brown
today are tinted green and

hyacinth
the light darts

with the quickness
of the word

bird

NAMING

I

In the wood I hear the beautiful
call of bird I do not know   I wish
I knew the names of birds
and could identify them by their songs

It would be so much nicer to say
I heard the warble of a wood pigeon
as the red floor of the woodland
stretched before me like an avenue
through the high rises of beeches and oaks

as I walk on the path and feel the soft cushion
feel my foot press down into the flesh of the duff

because
a name is
          reassurance
a comfort in the flesh
to hold

these songs in the trees
so something could be mine

          warble trill bell fluting?
something nearly right

II

The urge I feel is
to give things names but

   everything is already
named

The urge I feel is
to connect with this land
these plants birds songs
these trees

To name things would be
perverse

perhaps the place within
will always escape the name

In the mind one leaves leaves &
leaves
but on stone earth and grass one stays forever

I have a few trees on my tongue
oak   maple   birch

I have a few birds on my tongue
seagull   mallard   redbreast

I have a few plants on my tongue
rhododendron   English ivy   iris

I have started to see that nothing is itself   everything
turns to something else

like birchbark becoming *vesses-de-loup*
I prefer
   the sound of my wife's ancestors
   the ashes of their throat

like the rhododendron barks becoming
fighting pythons
and me gathering chestnuts for dinner in

a stream that dips below ground
and re-emerges often –
this life –
I no longer know

III

When I go walking in Malham
there's still that part of me that
   didn't
want to come

that doesn't
want to be in this land
of Karrimor jackets

All I can handle
is nature under fingernails
my grandmother planting
negro yams
shaping the land

All I can handle is the landscape within me
not scenery
spread out on a canvas

To have money
is to have time
To have time
is to have the forests
and the trees

I look at my baby
mindsliding
in the sticky
film of the bud
rubbing her thoughts
between
fingers

and knowing the
purple lips of the
involucres in her mouth

And me   am I living
my childhood all over
again?

For her a wood will not be
burned for fire coal
where the pig pen is
            where you hide from your Mama
            where you escape from scolding & rolling eyes
            where the duppies live
            where the madman lives
            where wild animals stray dogs
and the unwanted go to die

And me   am I living
my childhood all over
again?

a child's way
of pinching flowers
a child's way of touching buds
but what I had never known
this way of listening to the forest

Did Daisy
Miss Patsy's eleventh child
and my playmate
even know her name
was a flower?

In Porus life was un-
pastoral
The woodland was there
not for living in   going for walks
or thinking
Trees were answers to our needs
not objects of desire
woodfire

Catch butterflies
along the way to grandmother
on the other side of the yam field
Just don't do something foolish
like lose the money or
take too long
so the pot don't cook
before daddy reach home

There's a way of paying attention to plants
a way of listening to trees
a way to hold a flower in your hand
now that I'm here in a park in England

and I stop when called by the pistils of a tree
There is something in the pink
that speaks so clearly to me   saying
glad you stopped   I saw you
from far away

I don't even know
what *they* call it
but I want to know
what it tells me
about itself

its appearance
with thousands of others
on this tree
that up to April
seemed like death

Our parents and grandparents planted yams
potato slips   reaped tomatoes
carrots and so on
Then market then money
then food then clothes
then shoes to go to school

Now I'm practising a different way
of being with the woods   only
I try not to stray too far from the path…

The daisies glitter
at my feet

SPRING

Happy children
in predictable hordes

take the way home
that goes through the park
because the sun is out and
because of you
galaxies of sepals
changing into masked knights

DAFFODILS
(Speculation on Future Blackness)

It's time to write about daffodils
again to hear

a different sound
from the word

daffodil

Imagine daffodils in the corner
of a sound system

in Clapham
Can't you?

Well you must
try to imagine daffodils

in the hands of a black family
on a black walk

in spring

FINDING SPACE (1)

The smoke rises
under the tent
in Roundhay Park
the table is full
the two-pronged fork digs
into jerk chicken
    they drink and laugh
slap dominoes down on a table
A man and his partner walk a dog
    the dog is leashed
they walk across the field and
stare at the tent
that has been set up
at the food
table
at the people at the crowd
of people
who partying who touching
who laughing
who voice rising
They made it
    at last
to take up their space in
the park
with reggae music
barbecuing and big big laughter
People gather round &
everybody is touching
It is glorious
    at last
at last

One week later the gladiator knights
have turned to Cold War rockets
walking   up
the   hill
on
Coltrane's piano

RHODODENDRONS

This is the wood of snakes
the heads fighting in a primordial dance
The wet barks fuse forming knots
I see a monster   actually what   there is something else
    speaking
a deeper thing about me
they know more
about rhythms and dances
about what they have been
about the burly beech towering above me parading its fire

FINDING SPACE (II)

Darkness falling   I am beside the water tumbling
over rocks   a load I do not need to carry
I have gone round the usual circuit
up slope and down road and slope again
walking over fallen leaves   crush scratch black pulp
into the cocoon whose membrane has dissolved
to skeletal film

Still I walk   smelling the fresh wetness of grass
crisp dampness of the air
There are many dogs I must get past along the way
as always running past or towards me
stepping off the path to give them room
They lick me they mark me with their paws
How far can I go before I am no longer there

Back home there are cows goats and mules
in the bush   and humans planting

How far can I go before I am no longer there
This walking is not easy

And now I'm beside the waterfall
inside this cocoon
my feet have grown roots
in the meat of brown leaves and earth
falling water drones beside me
awakening Dunns River Falls
and the year I first saw the sea

If only I weren't out of place
how long I would continue my conversation
with this form of water
Then I could stay here for hours
looking at its swirl its thickness
all the waters I had never listened to before
in every direction of time
over every solid thing
my soul leaps towards
a pinch in the stream
where eddies converge under a rock
There is my soul   *there*   I have seen it today

ON THE FIRST DAY OF AUTUMN

I give myself permission
to go outside
so nature can have a different look
and a different sound

a different sound in the stream
running over stones

a different look
in the floor of yellow leaves
of autumn just begun

I allow myself to listen
to have rest
in squirrels that run above my head

On the first day of autumn
I think about a tree   uprooted
and thrown down   that has sent
some of its roots back down into the ground

walking my mind in the dug-out road
of this tree   in its bole
of rotting leaves

this is the farthest I have come
to the edge of the world

a human walking on a tree
hanging my mind from the tussling odours
of mulch bark and rain

from a latticework of limbs
and roots exposed in a hanging grimace

This is the farthest I have come
to the edge of the world
to the edge of the work of
making the land home

so land
can have a different look and
a different sound

not of angry dogs and knives
but the sound of
my feet pressing down
into the flesh of the leaves

GOING STILL

I saw the rockets again
they came out overnight I stopped
and stared and then approached
and pulled a limb towards me
Let rocket be the word

for this surprising thing that will
in months' time be a green leaf
and a butterfly and a sack of seeds
like maracas dangling over ground
when they push forward their sprouts

I can hardly describe the excitement
of the green shaft which was hidden
like a treasure and now comes out
onto Earth's lip

A squirrel is no less a delight
a shock in the light of ordinariness

till a one-eyed mastiff — how could
I know the breed   but its shape
is the sound *mastiff* — jumps on me
having run down the slope beyond which
I was nothing but these future sprouts

   Zelda

the woman her owner
does she deign
to say good morning hello

I even think a handicapped dog
is a person in ways I cannot be

These days I cannot write poetry so
I come to the woods to reduce the speed
of my head   I'm in one of the better parts
it's mostly the matting of dead leaves

that one sees in a kind of broad avenue
stretching upwards from the lake
It's scattered with twigs in the shape of trees
the branches are falling away

and the silence here is a silence that is neither
emptiness nor fullness   the squirrels foraging
at the roots are silence
Why does nobody do nothing?
Why does nobody sit on the roots and watch?
Everyone is going
somewhere
Why do I still come despite the dogs?

The sun explodes into fine lines of light
that crawl over the grass
they weave a net of flowing water
as a squirrel darts up a tree
running through the fire

LISTEN

to the voice of the woods the chlorophyll
moving in the store box of the cedars
listen to the snakes of branches the weight
of water glistening on barks of birches

close eyelids and see dancing light
and shadow of dancing see footsteps
sliding over the litterfall a leaf
has scraped another

I do not understand the woods
something is always lurking
under the dead leaves
   somewhere
between the roots in the green
shade of a bark on a limb
in a fallen bird's nest

close eyes listening try
to name the songs that play
from small twigs and needles
falling to pods of acacia
try to be the parts of the forest
learn their names by breathing

and I glance over my shoulder
now and again not persuaded
that someone has not stumbled
off the path and into the bush
behind me but it's only
the noise of the woodland

now I am walking through the forest
now I am penetrating the slow
composition
of what makes me

standing
spreading
deepening

BLACK WALKING

In the mist I see
long lines of Blacks walking
death walks to slave ships
Black footprints
on cathedrals and monuments
of the city

I dream Black immigrant feet
my family on the move working
second third fourth jobs

Is that why
   hiking feels strange to us
   walking without purpose
   going up then down
   arriving at the same spot

Or maybe there is
a purpose   something
to find in the peaks

people who came here
long before
whose stories are in the land
they claim isn't yours

Is walking a reclamation
a moving slowly enough to say
this is a land you can take your time with

these peaks are safe   I won't need to run

AMONG THE GREAT OAKS IN AUTUMN

among the oaks
my skin is a type of bark

I give birth to rocks
the same thing that happens

to me happens to them
a leaf will flutter down

my roots and into another world
turning to ghosts

creeping back as the light goes low
I am painted dancers sprouting

from the vines
the strings of my body vibrate

to the strings of the rain

BUT WHAT ARE THESE WOODS ANYWAY?

This morning I stood looking away
as I listened to three dogs charge at me

I can't even tell you what they looked like
because I never saw them
only heard the rolling and growling
felt the breath   heard
the searching of paws
and there is nobody else like me
around here

I don't want my mother to say I told you so

I can tell you now
that there were two women
standing on the slope shielded by trees
These women call the dogs back
frantically   they can't control them
no they won't come back &
I feel their breath
I hear their breath   on my calves

Meanwhile all that time
I just stand there pretending
to look into the distance
I am actually looking into the distance
while I pray to god

Let I   not be
a disfigured shape or body

don't even know *what kind of dogs* they are

The walk through the forest was so peaceful
stepping in the black pulp   avoiding the runny bits
walking on the padding of leaves looking at
the squirrels jumping in the high branches
a sea of golden leaves falling into the lake
    magpies squawking

Sorry about that   he's only a puppy   you alright?

I continue
meaning to enter the peace again
heartbeat will take a while to return normal
The stream is breezy
a sound of branches
a moist slippery path
leading everything away

I'm alright now
Let me always be alright

I don't want my mother to say I told you so

LEISURE (1)

The sun splashes its light on the trees   their exposed skins glisten
Inside me a living thing is ripening   In this month of December
when night falls in early afternoon   it is a struggle to get here   and
now that I am here I am living

A sadness returns   A sadness for the boy I once was   What was my
poverty? Was it living in a space that was too little?
To go far might have been just
to enter the woods
behind the house
But there was a wall separating me from it

ALL OF A SUDDEN

It may be easier
to define "walking" based on
what it is not

seeing your body
through the eyes
of an other   standing
outside yourself
watching
self

I was going somewhere
I was on my way
I never allowed my body
to occupy space
the way these people do

Walking did not
exist
Perhaps it didn't need to

Perhaps walking   is pressing
one's weight onto things
Perhaps to not walk
is to make things breathe
in the depth of their silence

But perhaps walking is
breathing different
    with power and blossoms
and breeze

I went somewhere to collect
the breadfruit   buy Big Jill
of oil   three pounds of flour

I carried pardner money but
Ti kya
Ti kya you
Ti kya you go
a river
Mind you drown
You want me murder you
Chicken merry
hawk de near

It may be easier
to define "walking" based on
what it is not

always going
always hurrying
always time
short
always *chicken merry*
we don't have time
to waste
hawk de near

Now I am walking
I am not going

FINDING SPACE (III)

At the beginning you might forget
the skin you're in

Right now I share the path with dogs
and must remember here
the woodland is a place for them
and people come here
because of their dogs

To go walking in these woods is to face
a different idea of what human is

They all have names
like Toffie and Iffie and Reggie
They talk to them sweetly and loudly

From a distance a young woman shouts
to one who has run away
and is now sniffing at your feet
jumping with mudded paws
While she holds another on her leash
she is dragged along
and still three others trot
beside her

and you look in her direction
you don't know if you should meet her gaze
and as you swivel your head she darts a glance
you feel it more than see it

and she says something to one of the dogs again
and four dogs and two humans manage to pass each other
without touching
in a narrow track   One of us will go up on the banking
One foot will step into the soil litter and avoid the mud

This is not home where
when people see you   they *really*
see you
Something about the comfortableness
of bodies on bodies   with bodies
friction in space   eyes in eyes   held gazes
I am *in you* as an affectionate aggression

At home people see you
with their whole body

Here you share the path with dogs
and must remember
to go walking in these woods is to face
a different idea of what human is

beneath what used to be
I imagine   an impressive tree
        Split down its bole it
has sprouted green leaves   that will be rustling
        way into September
    At its base lying athwart the clearing
        is the severed part

The colour of brown has weathered to near-grey
    and the footfall of walkers has covered
the wood with a layer of dust & yet
    the part that has fallen among the spikenard
and hungry shrubs surges out of death

The raspberries feed on its breath
    and beetles thrive in the slurry middle
where the bole rots

Listen   there is nothing as exhilarating
as the feeling of life coming into you

Though people
    look suspiciously
stand and listen   do not go anywhere

we have been the workers
        just the workers

In the Congo   one man had a land
almost eighty times
the size of Belgium   as his estate

We have been property

When I talk about reclaiming time
I'm just thinking about my body
standing in the middle of this woodland
            and
doing nothing   nothing

AUTUMN

I enter
peel off the skin of my living room
It is October
and the light that falls
on the leaves
rises again
in a swell
while the red floor of the woodland
stretches like an avenue
through high maples and oaks
I press down into
the leaves   and wonder
how many seasons lie here beneath my feet
Here   there is no enclosure
only cells
making sounds on a frequency so low in
a world distant
from words
unpossessed   and full

Our ancestors' bodies were property. We've carried that knowledge with us. You will find it in our saying, 'Chicken merry, hawk de near'. Happy children, be wary; the hawk is always round the corner.

People who live in the wake of slavery and plantation, we know we must always be on guard. There's something about containment, self-policing, about not being able to totally let go. Deep down, we know that that ability to occupy your space, to look at the world from inside yourself – rather than at yourself from the outside – is also about time. To occupy space is to occupy time.

Even as a child you internalise that. That your life is less deserving of time than the lives of others. That for you, time is never *to be wasted*. That your life is marked by doing, working. And at a certain point this word begins to hover above you, around you. You hear it on television, you learn it as a concept; you can't remember when or where you first heard it. Leisure.

Only certain people have it. Do they have it because they can name it, the way Westerners name ideas and turn them into money?

And now you must unlearn this learning
learn to carry your body with the confidence of those entitled to time.

THOSE WHO CAN AFFORD TIME

Who wanders
   lonely as a cloud
with three golden retrievers?

Not me   no   not me
I could never understand this poetry

never understand what the poem was saying
and how this could be
poetry for me

when my English teacher drilled
the imagination of a white man's country

didn't know how but somehow I knew
this wandering was not
for me because

  ours was not the same kind of time
     our wandering never so accidental
so entire so free

as if nothing was coming   as if no hawk was near
as if they owned the land and the mansion on it
as if tomorrow and forever was theirs

as if they had the right to take their time
   because
everything about them so refined   so secure
   so clean

So Wordsworth's poem never made sense
   I'd never stop to listen to the poems about trees
& mushrooms & odd cute things
& birds whose names I could never pronounce

My poetry was Tom the village deejay
more material   I said
    than the woods   than the lives of those who loafed

& bought their time
with money   I thought
those who had all the time in the world

ESSAY ON DOG WALKING (1)

In the woodland above us a man with his three
    I don't know the breed
They're big and so is their bark
scary for a baby &
babies don't come up here   but
ours does

We avoid making eye
contact
while she clings closer for reassurance

We could just   not come (like everybody else
who does not come
with their baby)

but if you saw the baby running & frolicking in the forest
and learning to play hide and seek behind the trees
and touching mushrooms and tapping the barks with her stick   sounding them
If you saw her smile and heard her laugh and knew that wood was her
    element...

I wish we could unknow this space
not care about it   stay home in our flat
    then everything might be easier

Think about these three big dogs
        and their roaming and how they own the hills and the woodland

But I know   you know
already   they don't expect to see
us in this area
no   not *round here*

44

We're not walking with the same codes   are we
I'm sure you realise that I   don't come here
    walking swiftly in the hills with water boots whistling calling shouting

but perhaps we might come   couldn't we come   to these woods
to find something that can only be found here?

ESSAY ON DOG WALKING (II)

One dog runs at me
I think fierce
I think big

I think stone
can survive an attack
    so I turn into stone

I must not be attacked
outside my
own home

by dogs
    I do not know

Another one comes at me
    from the opposite direction
and the jaw of uncertainty
    widens

It's OK
The man from yesterday
I fanned his dog away
from the baby's pram

His partner emerges   through branches
hands leashed   up slope
stumbling
Professional dog walkers
This is where they come to park the van

I walk a few metres
In the corner of my eye   a cloud
    dog rushing again

This time the dog is sicked
on another man
inside my body
another man
starts running
    before
        I open soundless mouth

It isn't just fear for my skin
            it's terror
            anger
struggling with each other
and neither can win   so

    I tell you   I say
to keep your
    dogs away from me!

'They won't hurt you'   she says
taken aback by my panic
Afterwards I will wonder about this
    Were the dogs that threatening
    Did I need to be so afraid

I walk toward the bus stop
    All morning I've been thinking
    about Brathwaite's *Short History of Dis*

where Cerberus is a Jamaican dog trainer
who tortures his dog so much
it whimpers in terror

In a reversal of Dante it's the man
that barks   becoming beast
while the dog cowers

There are things in our cells
hidden from view but
working the thatness of our bodies

His action is not just cruelty
Torturing the dog   training it
to be a bad rhatid dog is
his attempt to exorcise
a terror

The dog on the plantation
in the field
in the bushes
through the woods   barking
    ripping
flesh
this mauling
of the Black body
the violence that made
White life possible

The pampering
the caressing
the spoiling
the doting
the fussing

over the dog
reminds him
his ancestors
were property
    less than these animals

There are things in our cells
hidden from view but
working the thatness of our bodies

Like in me
    the dog barking up a tree
    the dog barking at my heels
like the dog
    is more than
        the dog

MASOCHISM

a big strong dog terrorizes
   a gathering of black families
      celebrating in the park

            long after the beast
          has darted past my feet and
       my heart raised high
     from the power of its legs
    from the energy of that sound
  on grass

long after it has raced through
   the gap of tam-tams and picnic baskets
      and the panicked legs of scrambling fathers

        only long after
      comes a call
    for Reggie
to come back

I don't know what the man has seen
   of all this
      nothing no doubt
         does he sense the tingle of fear
            standing there
               in the field
                  of dazed bodies?

I continue walking
        my heart falls back
    to this joy of grass birds flowers
my steps spread evenly once more

Eventually
    Reggie's man emerges
        from an unsuspecting
            clump of grass
                telling him to come on!

            I am walking
        my aim to look easy
      as if nothing squeeze in
    the feelings
of skins

of past deep down
    that knows the dog only
        as an attacker
            a marker of boundaries

every day I torture myself
    it's the price I pay
for walking
    here

ON PROPERTY

I

A white woman is walking her dog in Central Park   The
    dog is off its leash
though signs say dogs must be leashed at all times   A black
man asks her to leash
her dog

          An African American man

She is   confused and afraid

    even in violation
of the rules
    I have authority over this space and   you

The woman shouts at the man   the man films the scene
the woman shouts even more

I am going to tell them
an African American man
is threatening my life

repeats this line to operator

She has lost control of her voice
is shrieking   with fear
even as she clutches thrashing dog

She is   confused and afraid

The   *African American*
the space
the violation
The *African American*
man

How ordinary for her
to destroy

this body
How ordinary for her

to erase
this body
space

On this day
Floyd is also dying
with a foot on his neck
exhaling
his last breath on concrete
calling for Mama

II

He does not forget this
The park too is a death zone
              ancient

he puts on his glasses
          he's going out
          of place

he hopes
to soften his look of threatening   he hopes
that as he walks this way

those little round
 nerdy
            eye-
        glasses

will make him small   enough
to those vulnerable to this
type of body

perhaps it's the eyes
    the eyes not seen too much

III

He goes into
            the woods
with desire

he hears birdcalls
            he remembers

the park too
is a death zone

he does not
forget this
                    ancient feeling

what the park is

(A Black Man Enters the Woods)

I must be careful   she firsted me into the track
hold back

walk
slow

look at these black stumps   the squirrels
jumping

other beings seeing
you in their dreams

leave the track
walk far   be not

threatening
It's sundown   &

you share the land with squirrels
in their light

walking on carpet of beeches
in this flourishing

   life of leaves
It's sundown on the curtain of trees

   are you in
the right place

under the shade
where you grow

so careful
of your own gaze

so being here
& yet

so other in body
as if you walked in another

body & you tell yourself
    this shared constructed space

is all you have
to think & feel with   & somehow

you must keep on learning
how to be here

AN EVENING WALK WHEN SPRING IS ALREADY OLD

On the third of June
    I re-enter the woods

The trees' souls
    have bloomed into canopies

There is volume
    not just skeletons

Breeze passes into the placenta
    of this womb

There is hiding place
    in the trees

and the birds sing differently
    the leaves

have become a sea
    in my body

BLACK HOLES

Now the dandelions
have mostly gone
It is no longer the starry expanse
I had seen
a month ago
in the thickness of April

.

The blood flow
is slowing down   the ravens sit
on the glaucomotous eye
of the field

RHODODENDRONS ON THE RIVER

who dies like this

tranquil
and assured

in the earth that returns
for a castle

the bird sings
    my first evenings

I am waiting
    for my father

again
    it sings

enveloping evenings
the rhododendron roots

    a question
wrapping this attempt to think

    in an unending snake of time

WITHIN FULL OF CANOPIES

The light on the lake darts
like a snake
I am everywhere
in the breeze

and on some there of a memory
the branch forks into two roads
my tree a stolid bole
shooting towards its first limb
then upwards to canopies

I am going home
to children breaking heads of
ripe corn in the field
while an old mother
heads down into the ravine
chopping shrubs and nettle out of her way
The juice and sap of stalks claim the land

The stifling smell of chlorophyl
is comforting in a guinep tree
where
there is no past or future
a world silent and waiting
    though it is pain
it is silent and waits

The juice of oranges and guineps
travelling with a sound the boy can hear
vines coming to possess the earth and roofs
and tongues bursting like lily buds
in his belly

CLIMBING TREES

These beeches are unclimbable
no furrows for feet

At home I knew a tree
by climbing it

Lost inside the guinep branches
I felt close to God

and I was hidden
in a place before birth

a womb
nearing the sky

For hours I would
turn into something else

one of those brown or green lizards
living up there

The limbs of an old guinep tree
are suspended walkways

you travel with your belly
with your thighs   with all your feeling

The thick muscular limb is a road
you hug   your back is a caterpillar's

legs knowing
the skin of the tree

insteps rubbing
the green moss

Travelling above the earth
I go searching for something

both tree and lizard have
to see things down below

things that never see them
folks that never think they are seen

because they never learn
to see the world from trees

COMING FROM THE GROUND

The green lizard has walked down the road
of its high branch
Frightened   my hand turned feathers almost
let go

No doubt   in the beginning
it was much larger and terrifying

and no doubt   it carries that knowledge
inside its ribbed head   that looks down at me
its whole body   electric   a ridge of
green spikes   from end to end

I hug
a lower limb in respect

Questions are hatched in the litterfall of time
and I breathe all the things this creature's
remembering ridge has known
as it stares down
at me
coming from the ground

VEIN OF STONE AMID THE BRANCHES

after Giuseppe Penone

as-tu peur que ça t'écrase ?
il a l'air de poids
mortel pour une masse
d'hommes
mais en réalité
il n'en écraserait à peine qu'un seul
c'est le poids de l'homme
il ne faut pas que tu te rapproches
laisse-le se rapprocher de toi

think of a factory
and it appears
let the word *nuclear* press you
with its weight
    uranium trees mate in nuclear forests
make trailer crane bulldozer
        fission

tree is
a rite of presence
tree makes nuclear reactors
shopping malls

tree is heavy with the weight
of everything
that   could   fall on you to crush you
but since this is a conjuring tree
but since this is a vodou tree
but since this is a hoodoo tree
but since this is a medium
psychic science tree

magic spirit tree
it will not
harm

you will stand under it and
feel the weight
but it will not be
you will stand underneath it and
close your eyes

and when you open them
you will be in the world again

close your eyes
and you will see
a vein of stone
amid the branches

FALLEN BEECH

The tree has fallen
It will probably take years
tens   hundreds to die
it will probably not die at all

We by contrast   when air stops animating
our bodies   it happens so suddenly
   That is it   there seems to be no life after it
at least we cannot see I mean really see
we cannot see the form
that we can take after that moment
in the stark reality of cells

when we fall
when air stops animating our limbs
and we die
that is it

I mean   I know we are still there in reality
when we go under
we too eventually turn into something else and return
as spores as wood as stone

But the tree   oh the tree
it keeps on   so visibly so unendingly

Consider this beech
its life already begins to multiply
worms pullulate in the hairs of the roots
the bark begins its slow transformation into diamonds
and as for the limbs
news of their death has not even reached them

Each root each cell each leaf each flow of sap
running through it
starts forming towers   new cities   us

We seep slowly into the cold
unbodying ourselves
But this beech already is reborn
gathering and amassing
all this juice and all this joy
in the sweet being of the earth

in this mountain
of some millions of years to come
where the obsidian   or some rock never before formed
remembers that I too was here

TREENESS

a tapestry of earth suspended
  in a forested temple
    beneath the roots
      the sheer face of a cliff
music from a rock gong
  among the snakes
    of the rhododendrons
      trembling at the blackness
of their skin a human walking
  among the birds
    past the barrier of time
    a climb away from land
where we punish ourselves
  because there are no trees
    because the woodlands
      have been cut down &
land has no time for itself
  If my thoughts can become
      ageless let them travel to a place
    called Infinite from
the words that kill time that kill
  things that kill vines let me lie
  in the infinity of a beetle in
    its meshwork in the muscles
that grow from its burrowing
    away from the noises
      of the crowd whose sounds silence
      the music of rhododendrons
who shun the temple of the rock gong

and the sacred hanging tapestry where
        the birds' thoughts echo
            Dear tree let me lose
my head and find it in the
    hairs of the birches
            in the air where my feet meet the
                the river that blossoms
from their exposed veins

THE SQUIRREL HOUR

A grey squirrel appears
under a beech sapling
smells its way closer
   In the matted spikenard
I am not threatening   it seems
the squirrel could almost
come to my feet
except
it catches my
   too human gaze
   shifts course
goes off a different way
and as it goes
every unspooling of the limbs
is a tenderness drawn inside me
   a blanket of silk
the spell of its camber
disappearing into plush mounds of litterfall

A TREE AND TWO HUMANS

The oak has rotted and is
    half alive
a squirrel clambers
    into its elevated cave
hundreds of years dead
    but some leaves have stayed

A couple arm in arm
has stopped to listen & look
I tone down my speaking   wait
for them to pass

a quick glance tells me
they are friendly

He says hello with his cave man voice
as if to say   I acknowledge you
we're doing the same kind of seeing
The partner smiles with her eyes

it is sundown   the squirrel hour
a horde of them at twilight
the chestnut pods glow in the dark

a raven also stands under the light
falling from the outside

SEAGULLS

When I get to them they are a colony
picking and squawking
a white bar lying on the wide field

I am blessed to see them

Then   one thud raises them into the sky
suddenly all those wings flapping in unison
I thought   what a beauty of some
unknown mind deciding a precise moment
when that multitudinous flap of the wings
should happen

I heard a noise a call a song and thought
a soft moan of a pigeon or dove? And then I saw it
above   a machine flying among the birds

I swivel my head round and round
but there is no one

So the sound was no moan
of a pigeon or caw of a raven
but a motor purring where the birds fly

Some human extends its will over things
Some human has made a gadget
and doesn't remember the birds
no   doesn't remember the birds

ROOTS

summer's day in quartz
ships' smooth skin on water
broad beach of volcanic sores
a thousand selves
and more

around me the rocks are
petrified alligators
gorgeous in black blisters

they butt the wind
as if they could move again
and pounce with the tide

I watch their swift running
from among the dunes
and listen to the waves
rustle the leaves of stone

to my right the silver sand sings
a lone seaside pine on a butte
blooms into a parasol
my heart is a jumble of rocks

inside there are so many creatures
so many seas
are those reptiles running
another time moving
are the rocks a sea within a sea

I will sleep in the sand
in the rocks and the quartz that oozes
like sores from the skin of granite

the silver sand sinks and
I do not know how far I will go
and the rocks and the sea sing
about a time that is within
not mine   in a voice too low

to my right the tropical sunshine
and the lone seaside pine
surrounded by the smouldering wicks
of rock samphire   I have run to be here
far from home

the rain stings my knees burn
from clumps of fescue
as I look out to sea

can we not hear from
this height ten volcanoes
spitting their lava to create the islands
and beside it we have a place to live
in God's dust

I want to know more
about the roots that nourish the rocks
that keep them tall and flourishing

The African Methodist Episcopal Church (AME) was founded in Philadelphia in 1816. Emmanuel AME Church (Mother Emmanuel) was established when the congregation in Charleston, South Carolina, met in secret until the end of the American Civil War.

In Saint Mary, Jamaica, the ruined building of an AME church can be found at the site of a former sugar plantation, in the dense forest near Kwame Falls. As stated on the plaque on its front wall, its leader was one Mrs. F. Aicheson. On the plaque is inscribed the date '3rd June '20'.

The land

We feel blood coming and going
says my guide   in roots

that ruins cover
Our blood is felt

in the underland of spirits
running through slavery and

ports of blood
connecting roots of AME

Philadelphia   Baltimore   New Orleans
Savannah   Charleston

where a white man
opens fire on a Black congregation

killing nine
running through these Saint Mary hills

and the Ebenezer AME
overgrown with bush

souls inside trees
in iron lignum vitae

wind and leaves
keep memory

the sea is right beside us
as well

humming people long dead
and these ruins standing in

time suspended

*

A strong place

Clap of the waves
against the cliffs below

the theme
of the stone's song

outside the curtain
of woodland

Here on this rocky
hillside where the

underworld temple
stands land

screams sneakily
inside its stones

Women are born
from rock

with backs
hardly remembered

for the men they carried
in war and rebellion

What happened here?

The moss-blotched guango
says nothing

about the Black understory
Its pioneer Mrs F Aicheson

is covered by ruins
by the lichen mat   by the guango sapling

piercing through the belly
of the sanctuary

*

Dis place: A Song for the AME and Mother Emmanuel

How   Lord

did you teach the soul of the slave
to grow into a tree

the murdered body to burst
out of the ground like cedar

the Mandinka warrior to rise
from the root of lignum vitae?

If Charleston's souls found new bodies
could they have found them here?

found muscles   breath
hands and arms in these trees?

I listen across time

their hallelujahs
in the lives of wood

the secrets stone
does not silence I listen

Here they have stolen away
A god decided

they should stand
that their arms should wave a memorial

in the land that unburies the dead
They sing

Out of *A.M.E.* an otaheiti grows
a guango rises from the body

of praying mothers

       *

Epilogue

Kwame Hills   Saint Mary   Jamaica
sleeping land of spirits

The pathway through the bush
rises rigid and sheer

Succulent lianas
and cocoa leaves pause
as if waiting

The fisherman my guide
walks behind

We're in a land
of uncurated people

ESSAY ON DOG WALKING (III)

Shout at *me*!
Let me feel like a person

ESSAY ON DOG WALKING (IV)

The name Cynic derives from Ancient Greek κυνικός (kynikos), meaning "dog-like". It seems certain that the word dog was also thrown at the first Cynics as an insult for their shameless rejection of conventional manners.

I'm troubled by this normalcy

in which the dog
gets everything it wants

      *

They are babies   people
   owned objects

I have no idea what they are called
the numerous breeds

But why are you estranged
from yourself

      *

Would you understand
the way   she looks at this dog

makes me uneasy
the way she   speaks to it

the way she speaks to it
as a person
when the dog has strayed
   a baby disappears

it's hard to even
wrap your mind around it

the dog an extension
into other bodies

what is a comfortable walk
   over the field

   for you?

         *

It is dark in here
under the trees

I must tell you
my body is from a different time

I'm walking on my own
just to smell the branches
breathe the leaves

listen to the birds in the trees

I am here &
no dog runs beside me
I've left my children at home

Let us think about
what it is to go walking

to be a body that walks
works   here

LOGWOOD

A stone frieze adorns the face of the Clothworkers Hall at the University of
Leeds.
It depicts Black people bearing the trunk of a tree.
          The trunk is heavy. I am on a 'Heritage walk'. The guide, a
historian, explains that the wood represented
                    is logwood.
                    It is an autumn day in 2019.

Upon returning on August 11, 2020 to the Clothworkers Hall, a quiet, still
      day during the pandemic, I see no frieze. Is it somewhere there?
                    I had seen it…

Today
each of the building's three triangular gables carries
a sculptured relief.
          The first is of a branch
             of the indigo plant, with its pods;
                    the second represents the flower head
             of a teasel viewed at close range; the third,
finely chiseled overlapping woods
from the logwood tree.

Logwood – prime dyewood and staple of the dyestuffs industry
          comes mainly from Central and South America,
          and from the West Indies.
Indigo and dyewood were important to the textile industry,
                              a primary activity in Leeds during the
          Industrial Revolution &
up until the late 20ᵗʰ century.

In the eighteenth century,
in the West Indies,
   the most robust importation of slaves and
   expansion of the sugar plantations
   was taking place. The Transatlantic Slave Trade was at its apogee.
Plantations also provided
      indigo and logwood,
      two essential raw materials for
Britain's textile industries. Profits
from sugar provided precious capital for their growth.

Where is that image of bare-backed men struggling with a log, their faces
exhausted from carrying the weight
& from the heat?

It is now a dream
 but so real
like a ghost

   *

the word logwood
a veil
opened and closed
I was again
on the red path that leads
into the woodland
surrounded by now
the tree of memory
a mysterious ladder of sens-
ation

I leap into
the spirit of the wood

with an awkward bound
the hand of the word
pushing me

in the courtyard
the word is a spirit
& in the word I hear

a forest of skins &
a distant hum

*

logwood

a tree I'm trying to remember
trying to retrieve the meanings of
logwood
from my grandmother's voice

in the walk we made often
down to the place called Gully
over hills and down to
Grung
where she planted yams
Mama
in this dead wood on the facade of
the Clothworker's Hall at
Leeds University

down in it   their breathing
in the crowd their breathing
grows clearer

I can hear them
in the bush

I would be a tree
my arm branches
waving to the life above me
blossoming in the sun

      *

I am awakening to the world
it was in Leeds that something stirred in me
the haunting of place
by place

how they haunt the facade of this building
how I came to meet their spirit here
in the stone

everything now changes place
every poem is
    that yam grung
its silence warm oil
    on my chest
its sound   partitioned
into temple and
cho-cho walk

down in the wood is their breathing
the noises are in the crowd
down in it their breathing grows clearer
in the spirits of the wood

in Black River
a ship is loaded
their blood is a human tree
their quantities float down the river
their blood is shipped from Black River
their blood is present at my birth
their blood is weighed in large scales
every poem is Black River

a tree I'm trying to remember
retrieve the meanings of logwood
from my grandmother's voice
in the walk we made often
down to the place called Gully
over hills and down to
Grung
where she planted yams
Mama
in this dead wood on the facade of
the Clothworker's Hall at
Leeds University but

down in it is their breathing
the noises are in the crowd
down in it their breathing grows clearer

*

Log

Where is the word
            land
                        where is the word
                                    history   where

    is the depletion of forests

                        The heartwood is heavy and extremely hard

            A shortage of indigo caused by the Napoleonic wars

22 December 1802   Leeds firm J. and J. Holroyd
                        writes, "10 tons Campeachy Logwood"

                    the firm of Fleetwood and Arguibel at Cadiz
                                            requesting
among other things

                                                bloodwood

campeachy

        a destabilising spirit

                        campêche

the tree is so known   the French West Indies

    sound   de- logic

comme campêche pou coutelas

'like campeachy to a cutlass'

                  campeachy

                  comme pêche

                  like a peachy

The coloniser is at home
      every   where

Comme campêche pou coutelas
    resilient
not easily broken
   surviving even
when given up for dead

          the plant used in certain traditional systems
                 of medicine

log-

                                 ging broken

                    histories

                        logs of dying

      logs

of erasures

                                  wherever they are now

how do I reach them

where do histories
               go
when the trees have been killed

             when the logs
have become the part
                      we cannot find

PLAGUE WALKS

I

The red floor leaps into my eyes
as the birds
enter space again

when was the last time you had   like this
entry into the green
hearing the birds stitch language
to language

Was it early morning yard
in Coffee Grove
before people drank tea
in condensed milk cans
when the chocolate on fire
dreamed in its oil

and Mammy said *look at that eh*
that noise is not the whirring of drones
Remember the morning where nothing
needs you   you see the birds fly again
the swans' awkward over-heavy wings
opening the sky

II

with patience
the layers peeled off

I come
and listen to the deep

things scrambled in
water

take not Coffee Grove
away from me

words that form eyes   ears
in which I escape

perhaps the price I pay
is a small stream bearing me back

to Dunn's River Falls
where I first saw the sea

that envelops all times
the air makes understanding hard

for feelings to touch more than skin
what a funny thing to *see*

the virus *memory*
as if seeing was smell

a feeling thin like breeze

III

The dandelions are fully out
Their glow is the aroma of
warm kerosene rising from
a Home Sweet Home lamp

The liquid smell
is a white tablecloth spread out
in the inside of my flesh
I hear the thud it makes
when one unfurls it

soft thud
the breathing of their light
that pours through
my skin and rises to seal me
in a bed of feathers
in a green wood
whose silence warms the body

IV

the gladiator buds everywhere
in the forest
ready to push forward
their leaves   galaxies of dandelions

so much life has missed this year
while we have been indoors

I came out and the horse chestnuts
had already blossomed

and all of spring
stood there

thick to the touch

v

when I see you round the corner
in the mist of running of a blink
I thought a tree standing there
in the path is no human
in Karrimor jacket

the birdcalls of the stream
go on
there   there the susurration

the body is there
on an empty park day
empty woods
daffodils and absent children

But what is the sound now of silent lyric
in this patch of daffodils

VI

flesh of evening
blood flows

listen to the wetness
in rhododendron

to the ovulation
of the river

people speak insides
things they have

measured
and counted

dogs run before
dancers

a Black dancer strikes
poses on the bridge

fingers touching
toes raised to the sky

jetés posed
he holds them

and his friend
photographs

round and round
the angles

two White men are
pulled into the woods

by their dogs
the rhododendron

snakes
long-bellied

of the wood
selves of land

selves of evening
selves of sound

VII

to stay alive I
reach out and hold another sunlight
then reach out and hold another night
in the shade of an old tree

VIII

The stream is breezy
a sound of branches
a moist slippery path
leading everything away
to Jamaica
where iguanas and a sugar plantation
awake to my ancestors' feet
as they meet
the moist earth of the river

an old fear of what you used to be
when you used to walk in another skin
and all the fear from another skin
that comes back over and all
from a deep down struggle
not to see the dog as an enemy

my navel string is planted in a land
of brightness and terror
where overseers follow with guns
on horses

in a land that
calls out to me
I *could* be yours

A French bulldog   £3000
A strong tone   What voice   What   in charge   What
Daisy!   Daddy Daddy   King Charles
spaniel!
scrunch
my wellies!   the ground moving
my money!
the children
running
They've passed
running   the presence   the in charge
The in autumn   leaf cover
the slur   the sludge
the going out   the being
in charge
the dog   a collection the creature a part a sticking to
a leash
a number
a mathematics of aggregational logic
I don't know what   if not   a leash

x

all of a sudden the tree protects me
there is a sea blowing
   in its leaves
foam dawning on a white beach

  a bud
a sheath
  a split
a multiplication of sprouts
leaves
poured out
like running water

DO YOU FEEL THEM LOOKING AT YOU?

For Malika Booker

Did I tell you
I do not come as often anymore

It becomes overwhelming
to be out of place and
I hear the ancestors saying we
have avoided the woods
They are writing with us sister

I hear the ancestors say
we have used the woods
we have needed the woods
we have tamed the sounds
of calabashes and squawking birds
became our invisible garments

They enter our space again
we enter the silence of real things
and know we are with them
reclaiming time
we are we are we are

Do you feel it too
this surge of the being
this world entering your skin
this yourself as the elements
this becoming woodland
this becoming stream
this becoming river

And yet do you feel you too
scared to come watching
your shadow you thinking of what
might be flying behind your head
you thinking what if
what if today
this time
am I going to keep on
being safe

How does it feel in
        your body
over there
Are you there
can you reach out

The ancestors remind us
    through each other only
through each other
only

of what is due to us
of our body as sound as water as wood as stone
of our body as river   here

Do you too feel eyes of the woodland looking at you
do you feel their eyes too?

FEAR OF MEN

Must we imagine the trees at dark night,
the moonlit fields and woodlands,
the banana leaves and their bizarre
anthropomorphisms?

Must we imagine the moon growing full
and strolling in the sky, the clouds
that suddenly veil the light,
covering the earth in darkness?

Must we imagine the moment a gust of wind
shakes the branches, and when,
awakened out of torpor, a patoo
begins to cry?

Must we imagine silhouettes rising, gigantic and black,
the involuntary step backward from a human shape
and the gasp one makes
at the idea of a duppy?

Must we imagine the night and its spirits?
Must we imagine that, because of fear,
of roaming men, more than of duppies,
imagining the night is all we will do?

CHO-CHO WALKS

there is no doing here
the only activity is life
greedily glutting
assured of its forever self
twigs fall in the silence
of Coffee Grove
where hearing is just walking
your shadow blending with those of the vines
Mammy carried a machete in her hand Spanish Bill
to part the succulent weeds to ask them to excuse us
the cutting and digging was for cocoyams
that we would roast in the afternoon sun
my machete was for feeling grown
a worker whose hands plough the soil
I cannot tell you the delight of coolness
the delight of walking under a cho-cho walk
of hiding for a child
becoming flesh of the flesh of the leaves
walking with caterpillars on all fours
when all we had was a machete
yam sticks and cho-cho walks
the grown-up boys had slingshots
made trucks from cardboard juice boxes
and real engineering was to build a hand cart
I settled for avocado wagons and cars avocado men
everything built from an avocado seed
the path that leads back into the cho-cho walk
leads through the undergrowth of maple trees
in Leeds the light is different but the same
the setting sun that dapples the leaves

is different but the coolness is almost the same
the bird calls are different but bird calls
are nouns and nouns are spirits
giving you sounds you need to hear

TWILIGHT IN ROUNDHAY

A bird glides slowly
touches down on the green
and people ribbonned in darkness
look up at the light
a view from inside a flower

Ahead a grackle walks
as if there was no tomorrow
a dog sprinting after tennis ball forms
a circle around me

Time makes holes in everything's skin
I dream the red sun of Coffee Grove
in this sky crisscrossed
by roads of smoke

to see a bird gliding in the milky wave
of the yam vines
    slowly to perch on the common mango tree
while the goats' hooves prance on rough asphalt
the shepherd's machete scrapes the ground
kerosene oil makes dark burnings in the air

The bird is comfort
a conversation going on
between me and all I see

I will learn to name this me
walking through the park
and that silence   the light above
the cold lines from aeroplanes

NOTES & ACKNOWLEDGEMENTS

Thanks are due to Michael Schmidt and John McAuliffe, my publishers; to Lucile Allen-Paisant, my partner; to the University of Leeds poetry group (John Whale, Vahni Capildeo, Malika Booker, Rachel Bower, Charlotte Eichler, Lydia Kennaway, Mick Gidley, Carole Bromley); and to Jacob Ross, Khadijah Ibrahiim and Kimberly Campanello. Special thanks to Malika Booker, who has been a main source of motivation and support throughout this project.

The following people are foundational; with their support and belief over the years, they have helped to birth this work: Charles Henry Rowell, Gregory Pardlo, Shivanee Ramlochan, Curdella Forbes, Kwame Dawes, Jeremy Poynting.

Special thanks to Jemma Deer for inspiring the title of this book.

Thanks are due to the editors of the following publications in which some of these poems have previously appeared: *PN Review*, *The Poetry Review*, *Granta*, *Stand*, *bath magg*.

*

'Black walking' – Based on the words of Testament, as reported in Bridget Minamore, 'Black Men Walking: A hilly hike through 500 years of Black British History', *The Guardian*, 23 January 2018.